COPERN
GALILEO
AND
NEWTON

Contents

What is space science?   2

Nicolaus Copernicus   12

Galileo Galilei   30

Isaac Newton   48

Space science today   66

Glossary   76

Index   77

Space through time   78

Written by Jo Nelson
Illustrated by Martin Bustamente

Collins

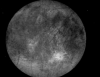

What is space science?

Space science is the study of outer space. By looking at other planets and moons in our Solar System, we can learn more about our own planet. By looking at other Solar Systems in our galaxy, we can learn more about our own Solar System. And by looking at other galaxies in outer space, we can learn more about the universe itself, including how it first began.

How has space science developed?

We've come a very long way in our understanding of space. We know the Earth goes around the Sun, but it took thousands of years for people to realise that.

In books and on computer screens we can look at detailed photographs of distant stars, but for thousands of years people could only see tiny bright dots in the sky.

Until 1961, no one had ever been into space. Now, around 500 people have been there, and there's a space station **orbiting** Earth where people can live and do experiments.

There are over a dozen unmanned spacecraft, known as **space probes**, exploring our Solar System and sending information about other planets and moons back to Earth. New discoveries are being made every year, and there's still so much more to find out.

Only in the last 400 years have people begun to realise how big the universe is, and just how tiny our planet is within it. But we wouldn't have the knowledge we have today without some very great minds daring to think differently and make astonishing discoveries.

That's where early space scientists come into the story. Except that they didn't call themselves space scientists. The word "space" wasn't used until the 1660s. Instead, people called the area above and beyond Earth "the heavens". The word "scientist" wasn't used until 1834 and the word "science" was used as a more general term to describe any knowledge gained through study.

Aristotle
*384–322 **BCE***

Ptolemy
90–168

Copernicus
1473–1543

Galileo
1564–1642

Newton
1643–1727

Sun, Moon and stars

Every morning, the Sun rises above the horizon. It moves
in an arc across the sky – high above our heads in summer,
lower down in winter – until it sinks and sets behind
the opposite horizon. That's how we see the Sun today
and how humans have always seen it.

It's hardly surprising, then, that for thousands of years people
believed the Sun really was moving around our planet and that
we were stationary in the middle. At night, people saw the stars
move across the sky and believed they too were rotating around
the Earth.

Wandering stars

The movements of the planets were harder to explain. There are
five planets that we can see in the night sky without a telescope:
Mercury, Venus, Mars, Jupiter and Saturn. They look just like
stars, but they move separately from the real stars.

6

Sometimes they look brighter in the sky because they have moved closer to Earth. Sometimes they look dimmer because they have moved further away.

For a long time people just saw them as stars that wandered across the sky, rather than moving with the other stars. They became known as planets, based on the Greek word *planetes* meaning wandering.

This is the planet Mars. You can see how it moves in the sky.

The Earth-centred universe

Until the 1500s, most people thought that the stars in the night sky were at the edge of the universe and that the Earth was at the centre. The area around the Earth was known as the heavens. The objects in the heavens – the Sun, Moon, planets and stars – were known as celestial bodies, meaning "bodies of the heavens". They were seen as beautiful objects that would never change, but would keep on moving around the Earth for ever.

Aristotle and the heavens

The idea of the heavens rotating around
the Earth was described by the ancient
Greek philosopher Aristotle in around
350 BCE. He explained that the celestial
bodies – the Sun, Moon, planets and stars – were
fixed on to massive spheres, like hollow crystal
balls, with the Earth at the middle of them all.

Aristotle

They were made to rotate around the Earth by something
greater than themselves – something that people didn't really
understand, but that Aristotle called the Prime Mover.

Aristotle believed that the heavens were perfect. He thought
the most perfect shapes were circles and spheres, so he decided
that the celestial bodies must be spherical and that they must
move in circles.

The problem with planets

Aristotle placed all the fixed stars on one massive sphere.
He then tried to explain the wandering movement of
the planets by placing them on separate spheres within
spheres that could move at different speeds.

But this didn't explain why the planets were sometimes
bright and sometimes dull, or why they sometimes appeared
to move backwards.

Aristotle's universe

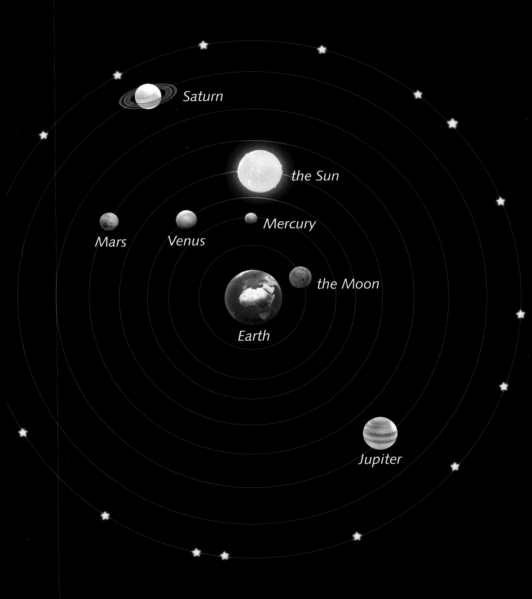

Saturn

the Sun

Mercury

Mars

Venus

the Moon

Earth

Jupiter

Ptolemy's solution

Over 400 years later in Egypt, philosopher and mathematician Claudius Ptolemy came up with another idea. He introduced little epicycles – circles on circles – that matched the movements of the planets more accurately. These epicycles meant that while the planets were each moving in a big circle around the Earth, they were also moving in their own little circles.

Ptolemy

The epicycles explained why from Earth the planets looked as if they were at times moving backwards. They also explained the varying brightness, as the planets moved nearer to Earth, then further away.

Each planet moves round in its own circle, as well as moving round the Earth in a bigger circle.

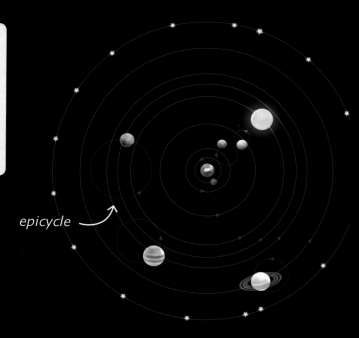

epicycle

A geometric model

Ptolemy used geometry – the mathematics of shapes and positions – to create his model. He started with the ideas proposed by Aristotle and other ancient philosophers, putting the Earth at the centre and having the celestial bodies moving around it. Then he used observations collected by astronomers over the previous 800 years to **fine-tune** his model.

Ptolemy didn't question the position of the Earth at the centre, and he never thought of using any movement for the planets other than circles. He kept adding epicycles on epicycles and shifting the centre point of circles, until he felt that he had an accurate representation of the heavens. His model could now be used to work out the positions of the planets and other celestial bodies at any time.

Ptolemy published his work in a book and included a list of 1,022 stars. The book was widely read and Ptolemy's explanations stood largely unchallenged for over 1,300 years.

Centuries after Ptolemy died, the Roman Catholic Church used his model as a true description of God's universe. Priests explained that the sphere of fixed stars was in fact Heaven, and that the Prime Mover responsible for moving all the spheres in the universe was in fact God. The model seemed so neat and obvious, few people thought to question it.

Nicolaus Copernicus

Copernicus

15th century Europe

In 15th century Europe, the Roman Catholic Church was at the heart of people's lives. Communities revolved around the Church. Their festivals and holidays were set by the Church calendar. Hospitals, schools and universities were mostly established and run by the Church. Even what you were allowed to think, eat and drink was guided by the Church.

a religious event in Venice

The Church and Astronomy

The Church encouraged the study of the universe. Gazing at the sky on a clear night was seen as a wonderful way to admire God's creation, and it had practical uses too. The Church relied on Astronomy for its calendar. Each year, Church astronomers used the stars to work out the exact date when day and night are equal lengths. From this they could set important dates such as Easter.

At university, Astronomy was an important subject. Students were taught Ptolemy's model and they learnt how to use his calculations to predict the movements of the celestial bodies.

students studying Astronomy

Young Copernicus

One student of Astronomy was Nicolaus Copernicus. He was born in 1473, the fourth and youngest child of a wealthy merchant family in Toruń, Poland. His mother and father both died when Copernicus was young, and he went to live with his uncle, Lucas Watzenrode.

Watzenrode was a priest who later became a bishop. He made sure Copernicus had a good education, sending him to a cathedral school, then to the University of Krakow. It was in Krakow that Copernicus first studied Astronomy – and how Mathematics could be used to work out the movement of the stars and planets.

Watzenrode wanted his nephew to have a successful career within the Church, as a priest and maybe even a bishop. So he sent him to Bologna to study canon law – the rules stating how churches should be run and how members of the Church should behave.

Copernicus used this opportunity to study Philosophy and Astronomy as well. He became assistant to Bologna's Professor of Astronomy, Domenico Maria de Novara. One of Novara's jobs was to predict future events in the sky, such as **eclipses** of the Moon. Copernicus joined him on his nightly observations of the sky, and it was there he made a new discovery.

Domenico Maria de Novara and
Nicolaus Copernicus studying the night sky

Testing Ptolemy

Several astronomers in Bologna at the time were puzzled by their observations of the night sky. They were using Ptolemy's model to calculate when an event should happen, only to discover that the timing was wrong. Copernicus decided to put Ptolemy's model to the test himself.

With its reddish orange glow, Aldebaran is one of the brightest stars in the sky.

The event he chose was when a bright star named Aldebaran was due to be blocked from view by the Moon. Copernicus calculated when the Moon should move in front of the star according to Ptolemy's model, then he looked at the night sky. He saw that the timings didn't match – the bright star wasn't hidden by the Moon on the night Ptolemy's model said it should have been – which meant that Ptolemy's model was wrong!

Clues from the past

Copernicus spent three years in Bologna, then two years studying Medicine in Padua. The plan was for him to be a physician to the bishop and other men of the Church, but while he was in Padua, Copernicus researched other people's views on the universe.

He discovered to his excitement that some of the ancient philosophers had believed in a different model of the universe; one where the Earth wasn't at the centre. Some even suggested that the Earth moved around the Sun.

Copernicus's watchtower

Copernicus finally passed his canon law exams and returned to Poland. In 1512 he went to work at the cathedral in the town of Frombork.

The telescope still hadn't been invented in Copernicus's time. All his observations were made by looking up at the sky and using simple, ancient instruments. He could measure distances and angles between the celestial bodies and predict their movements and positions, but he could never see them in any closer detail.

Swapping the Earth and the Sun

Copernicus made lots of calculations and drew different diagrams. He tried out a model where the Sun and the Earth swapped places, so that the Sun was in the middle and the Earth was moving around it, just like another planet. He realised this model could match his observations of where the planets are at different times.

But how could the Sun be stationary in the middle of all the planets, when it clearly moved across the sky every day? Copernicus solved this problem by suggesting the Earth also rotates on its own **axis** once every 24 hours. It may look as if the Sun is moving, but in fact it's the Earth that is turning on itself.

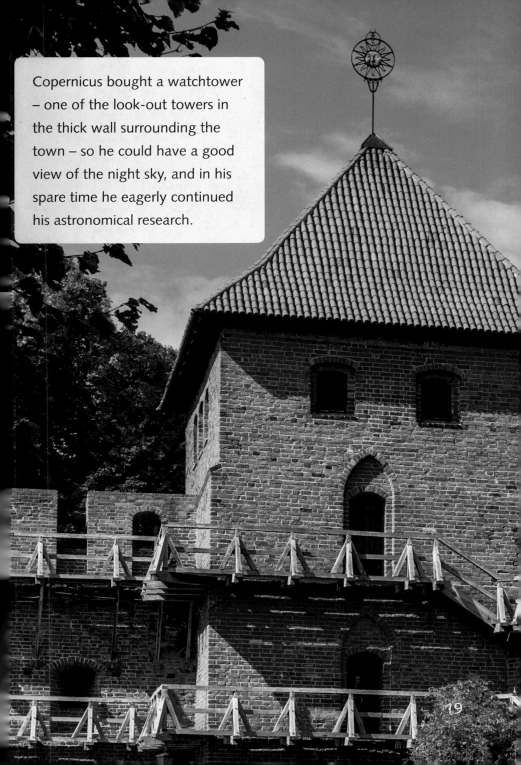

Copernicus bought a watchtower – one of the look-out towers in the thick wall surrounding the town – so he could have a good view of the night sky, and in his spare time he eagerly continued his astronomical research.

Copernicus's model

Here's how Copernicus imagined the universe
worked. The Sun is near the centre of
the universe. All the planets, including
the Earth, move around the Sun.
The distance between the Earth
and the Sun is tiny compared
with the distance from the Earth
and Sun to the other stars.

Only the Moon
circles around
the Earth.

The stars and the Sun don't
move. They look like they're
moving because of the daily
rotation of the Earth.

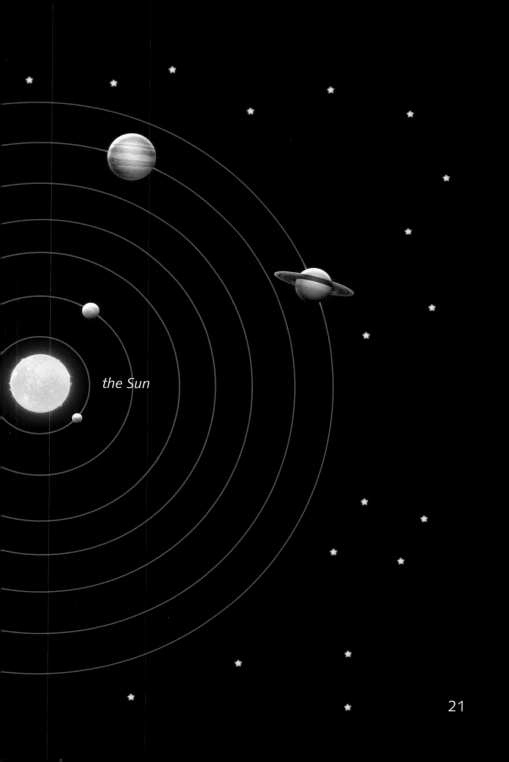

the Sun

More epicycles

Unfortunately, the one aspect he didn't think to question was that movements must be circular, so he still needed to add small epicycles to replicate the exact movement of the planets.

Arguing his case

At first, Copernicus didn't share his ideas. He knew they'd be laughed at by most people. How could the Sun be in a fixed place when everyone could see it moving across the sky every day? And how could the Earth be moving when it appears so still at our feet?

If Copernicus was going to convince anyone that he was right, he was going to have to come up with some good arguments. Ptolemy had said that the Sun moves alongside the planets, but Copernicus argued that it made more sense to put the Sun in the middle, since then it could light up the whole universe at the same time.

The Earth is moving

Ptolemy had written that the Earth couldn't be moving, or else everything on it would fall off as it spun round. Copernicus argued that we can still feel like we're at rest when we're moving.

Copernicus compared the movement of the Earth to the movement of a ship. When you're floating along, it's easy to think that you're the one who's still and that everything outside is moving. In the same way, he argued, we can be living on a rotating Earth and moving with it, while having the impression that it's the rest of the universe that's moving, not us.

Ptolemy had also said that a moving Earth would cause the clouds and birds in the sky to be left far behind. But Copernicus saw no reason why the air around the Earth shouldn't move along with it, just like the land and water does. Then the air would bring the clouds and birds along as well.

The stars are really far away

Since ancient times, people have been aware of an effect called "parallax" that can be used to work out how far away an object is. An example of parallax would be walking past a mountain with a tree in front of it and noticing that the position of the tree has changed in relation to the mountain.

It's not really the tree that's moved, it's the person looking at it who's changed position. The nearer an object is to the viewer, the more it appears to move in relation to things in the distance. The further away an object is, the less it appears to move.

The ancient philosophers tried to measure the parallax of stars but concluded that there was none. Ptolemy claimed that this proved that the viewer's position wasn't changing, so the Earth couldn't be moving. But Copernicus looked for a different explanation. He worked out that if the Earth was moving and the viewer's position was changing, then the fact that you couldn't measure the parallax of stars must mean they were incredibly far away.

The stars can't be moving

If the stars really were so far away, Copernicus argued, it was highly unlikely that they could make a complete rotation of the Earth every single day. The distance they'd have to travel, and the speed they'd need to move at to cover the distance in 24 hours, seemed impossible to achieve. It was far simpler to assume that the Earth was turning on its own axis, and that the stars remained in one place.

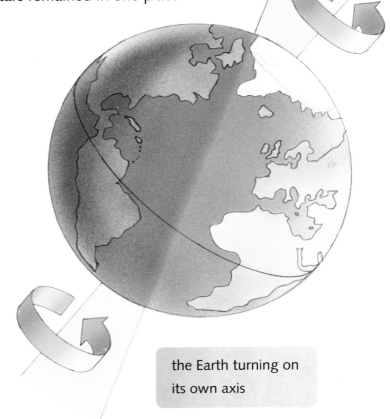

the Earth turning on its own axis

Keeping quiet

For a long time, Copernicus didn't dare publish his views; he only shared them with a close circle of friends. Copernicus had been a **pious**, hard-working member of the Catholic Church all his life and he didn't want to upset anyone by contradicting their vision of God's universe.

However, he did write down his theories and arguments and eventually, when he was nearing the end of his life, he was persuaded to publish them. A German scholar, Andreas Osiander, oversaw the publication of the book. Unknown to Copernicus, Osiander added a note in the front of the book stating that Copernicus wasn't describing the physical universe, only a mathematical model of it. He said that it was useful for making astronomical calculations, but that it wasn't actually true.

Copernicus would have strongly disagreed with this note, but he never got to read it. In late 1542 he was taken ill and in May 1543 he died, aged 70. A copy of his book is believed to have been shown to Copernicus on the day that he died.

Hiding from heresy

So why did Osiander add this note? He was probably doing Copernicus a favour. If the book had been presented as the truth, it might never have been published. Expressing a view that was different from the teachings of the Church was a serious crime known as heresy. People were imprisoned for heresy, and even executed.

As it was, a thousand copies were printed and circulated, creating great excitement and debate among scholars. Some were delighted; others were outraged.

This is how books were printed in the 16th century.

Banning the book

The Roman Catholic Church kept quiet at first. After all, the Church approved of studying Astronomy and using accurate models to calculate the movements in the sky. The book was even reprinted in 1566, but by then members of the Church were not happy.

Priests had been looking through their bibles and had found references to the Sun moving and the Earth standing still. They were using these passages to accuse Copernicus and his followers of heresy. Ultimately, Osiander's note was not enough to protect the book. In 1610, the Church officially turned against Copernicus's ideas and in 1616 his book was banned. After that, anyone even suggesting that the Sun was at the centre of the universe would have been in big trouble.

Galileo Galilei

Young Galileo

Galileo Galilei was born on 15 February
1564 near the Italian city of Pisa. He was
the eldest of six children and his father
was a well-known musician.

Galileo

As a boy, Galileo was sent to a monastery to be
taught by monks. He quite liked the idea of becoming a monk
himself, but his father wanted him to be a doctor. So in 1581,
aged 17, Galileo went to the University of Pisa to study Medicine.

One day, he wandered into a Geometry lecture by accident,
and found it fascinating. He asked his father if he could change
courses to Mathematics and Natural Philosophy – the study of
nature and the universe. His father reluctantly agreed. There was
much less money in Mathematics than Medicine, but he shared
his son's love of numbers.

Four years later, Galileo's father fell ill and could no longer
pay his son's fees. So Galileo left university and became
a Maths tutor. He also carried on with his own studies,
setting up experiments and inventing new equipment.

When Galileo was 22, he invented his own balance for weighing things in both air and water. The way he went about his research – wanting to try things out for himself rather than just rely on a theory – set him apart from other scholars at the time.

Head of Maths

At the age of 25, Galileo was appointed Head of Mathematics at the University of Pisa. It wasn't a very **prestigious** or well-paid job, but it helped him to build a good reputation. At this time Galileo didn't have a particular interest in Astronomy. He was more interested in exploring how things move.

In those days, most university professors based their teaching on theories written down by Aristotle hundreds of years earlier. Aristotle had developed theories on a wide range of subjects, using logical arguments to explain them. He had his own theory of how things move that stated the heavier the object, the faster it falls. This seemed to make perfect sense, but Aristotle had never actually tested to see if it was true.

Galileo refused to accept Aristotle's theory without proof. He began experimenting with different objects, rolling them down slopes and dropping them from heights. His results led him to discover that all objects fall at the same speed, regardless of how light or heavy they are.

If Aristotle's theory of motion was wrong, could some of his other theories be wrong too?

According to one of his students, Galileo
tried out his theory by dropping different
objects from the Leaning Tower of Pisa!

Galileo accepted a new job: Professor of Mathematics at the University of Padua. Padua was near to Venice and Galileo spent many days there. He was intrigued by the change in sea level between high and low tide. Galileo had heard of Copernicus's belief that the Earth moved, but he hadn't given it much thought before. Now he wondered whether the movement of the Earth could explain the tides. Perhaps it was the way the Earth moved that made the seas slop one way and then the other.

By 1597, Galileo had become convinced that Copernicus's version of the universe was the correct one. He admitted as much in a letter to the German astronomer, Johannes Kepler. Kepler shared Galileo's views and urged him to tell others, but Galileo feared how people would react so he kept quiet.

Supernova

In 1604, an extraordinary event gave both Galileo and Kepler more reason to doubt the ancient models.

A new star appeared in the sky.

Using modern telescopes, we know that a **supernova** looks like this. But to Galileo, it would have looked like a bright star.

Today we know that it wasn't actually a new star; it was a massive explosion taking place in a very old star. This kind of explosion is known as a supernova. Old stars are dim and hard to see but when they explode they're suddenly very bright and visible. That's why to Galileo and Kepler it looked like a brand new star had appeared.

Ptolemy and Aristotle had taught the world that the heavens were fixed and unchanging, but here was Galileo's first indication that they weren't.

The spyglass

In 1608, news of an exciting invention reached Galileo in Italy. It was a **magnification** device, created in the Netherlands and known as a spyglass. Two lenses – normally used to make glasses for people with poor eyesight – were positioned one in front of the other. Objects seen through the lenses looked three times larger than they really were.

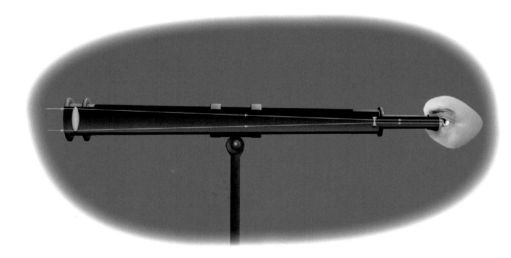

Without even seeing an example of the spyglass, Galileo rushed home to create his own. He quickly achieved the same magnification, but knew he could do even better. To get the lenses he wanted, Galileo had to make them himself, carefully grinding down the glass until it was exactly the right shape.

After hours and hours of hard work, he had made a spyglass that could make objects look ten times bigger.

He demonstrated its power from the top of St Mark's Tower in Venice, showing that you could see a ship through the spyglass two hours before you could see it with your naked eye. The Venetians were delighted and asked Galileo to supply their navy with spyglasses.

Next, Galileo used his spyglass when he looked at the night sky. For the first time in the history of mankind, the celestial bodies could be seen in greater detail and their secrets began to unravel.

Today Galileo's spyglass is called a telescope. The word telescope was first used by a Greek mathematician in 1611 to describe one of Galileo's spyglasses. It means "far-seeing" in Greek.

What Galileo saw

Galileo spent eight weeks of sleepless nights in his tiny courtyard pointing his telescope into space.

He saw that the Moon wasn't perfectly round as celestial bodies were supposed to be.
It had mountains and craters,
similar to Earth.

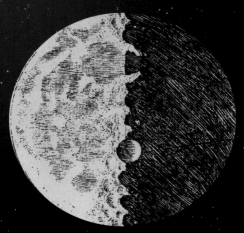

Galileo drew this picture of the Moon, after he used his telescope to look at it closely.

He saw that the Milky Way wasn't just a cloudy smudge across the sky but was made up of thousands of tiny stars.

He saw little star-like spots moving around the planet Jupiter and realised that they must be moons. Celestial bodies were supposed only to orbit the Earth, but here were some celestial bodies orbiting Jupiter!

Galileo was overjoyed. His telescope was making the invisible visible. He quickly wrote a paper about his wonderful discoveries, named *Starry Messenger*, and the first printing sold out within days.

There was so much more Galileo wanted to discover, but he still had to teach to earn a living. He decided he needed a patron – a wealthy nobleman who would pay for his research – and he knew just who to ask.

The Medici family

In *Starry Messenger*, Galileo named the moons of Jupiter after the powerful Medici family in Florence. He then sent a copy of his work and his finest telescope to Duke Cosimo de' Medici, along with a letter explaining how he would be grateful for a patron to fund his studies of the night sky. A few weeks later, Galileo was invited to become the Medici philosopher and mathematician.

Galileo was feeling much bolder now about his views on the universe. Aristotle and Ptolemy were wrong: Copernicus was right. Galileo just needed a way to prove it.

The phases of Venus

Copernicus had said that all planets moved around the Sun. If he was right, then Venus should change shape in a similar way to the Moon, since from Earth you would only see the part of Venus that was lit up by the Sun and facing you.

As Venus moves around the Sun, different parts of the planet can be seen.

Here, Venus is lit up by the Sun.

Here, only part of Venus is lit up by the Sun.

To the naked eye, Venus is just a bright dot, but Galileo's telescope clearly showed it changing through time, from a small disc to a larger crescent. Galileo thought he'd discovered the evidence he needed to show that the Sun is the centre of the universe. Surely everyone had to believe him now?

Galileo's view of the universe

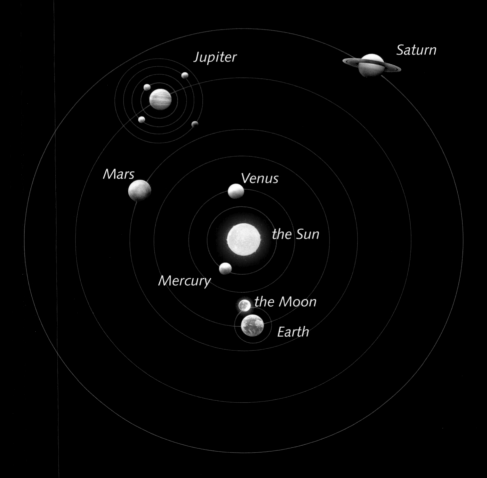

Silencing Galileo

Far from being convinced, priests and rival scholars turned against Galileo. Sermons in churches across Florence warned everyone to ignore Galileo's dangerous ideas. They thought he was deliberately contradicting the bible's descriptions of the Earth and Sun to cause trouble.

Galileo went to Rome to argue his case. Unfortunately it was 1616, the same year that Copernicus's book was banned, and no one listened to Galileo. The Church ordered him to stop teaching Copernican ideas. If he refused, he would be risking his life.

Rome

Galileo felt deeply frustrated. He believed in God and thought himself a good Catholic, but he couldn't see why the Church wouldn't accept the truth. To him, it didn't matter whether or not the way the Earth moved matched the exact words of the bible. The bible was for teaching people how to go to Heaven, not how things moved in the universe.

Unfortunately, the Church didn't agree. Galileo had no choice but to keep quiet – at least for the time being.

New Pope, new hope

Seven years later there was a new Pope, Urban VIII. Pope Urban
had always admired Galileo's work and so Galileo went to visit
him to discuss the nature of the universe. Galileo felt that
the Pope was on his side. He was told that he could write about
Copernican theory, so long as he presented it as just a theory,
not the truth.

Galileo's book

Galileo was delighted. He began writing a book that put forward both Ptolemy's model of the universe and the Copernican model. He included some of his own observations too, that he'd made through his telescope, and presented the book as a conversation between three people.

In 1632, his book was published. Galileo anxiously awaited a reaction, hoping that the Pope would be pleased.

He wasn't. It's possible that the Pope never actually read the book, but he was told by his advisers that it mocked the beliefs of the Church and this turned him against Galileo.

Galileo was ordered to Rome and put on trial on the suspicion of heresy. His crime? Believing that the Earth moves around the Sun.

44

Guilty

Galileo was found guilty and sentenced to life imprisonment. He was also forced to publicly withdraw his support of Copernican theory. At the time, Galileo said that he had to abandon the idea that the Sun was the centre of the universe, but he knew he was right.

House arrest

Galileo's punishment was later reduced to permanent **house arrest**. He moved back to his villa on a hillside outside the city of Florence. By now, his eyesight was failing so he could no longer study the night sky. Instead he wrote another book about his earlier work on how objects move. He managed to get this book published in the Netherlands in 1638. Four years later, Galileo died.

Isaac Newton

Young Newton

Just 11 months after Galileo's death, Isaac
Newton was born at Woolsthorpe Manor,
an old farmhouse in the tiny English village
of Woolsthorpe. He spent much of his childhood
alone, with lots of time to think. His father had
died before he was born and his mother had remarried
and moved away, leaving Newton with his grandparents.

Daily life in Woolsthorpe mostly revolved around farming sheep,
but animals didn't interest Newton. He was interested in
the patterns and rhythms of the world. And he didn't play
like most children, he experimented instead.

Newton

Newton's home,
Woolsthorpe Manor

Measuring the Sun and the wind

While other boys were playing chase and climbing trees, Newton was investigating the Sun and the wind. He noted where the shadows fell as the Sun moved across the sky and made his own sundial on the outside wall of his house. It worked so well, the villagers used it as they walked by, to check the time of day.

Newton made kites that could catch the wind perfectly. He measured the strength of the wind by seeing how much further he could jump when the wind was blowing. And when a windmill was built in a nearby town, Newton carefully made his own working model of it.

In the classroom

At school, Newton paid little attention to his teachers and was bottom of the class. The other students teased him for being odd and weedy. Then one day he was kicked in the stomach by a bigger boy. Newton fought back – and won. After that, he was determined to do better than the others. He started concentrating in lessons and trying harder with his school work. It wasn't long before he was top of the class.

On the farm

But Newton's education was interrupted when his stepfather died and his mother returned to Woolsthorpe. She wanted Newton to become a farmer, so she took him out of school. The problem was Newton was hopeless at farming. One day

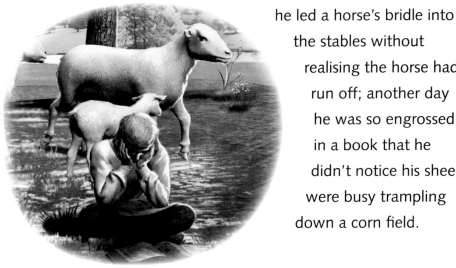

he was so deep in thought that he led a horse's bridle into the stables without realising the horse had run off; another day he was so engrossed in a book that he didn't notice his sheep were busy trampling down a corn field.

Rescued by university

It was Newton's uncle who rescued him by suggesting he might go to university. At the age of 18, Newton got a place at Trinity College, part of Cambridge University. He never went back to farming.

Newton at Trinity College, Cambridge

Not Aristotle again!

At university, many subjects – including Maths, Astronomy and different branches of Science – were grouped together under Philosophy. Newton was eager to learn first-hand the way the world worked, but instead the professors still focused on the ideas and models of the ancient philosophers.

Newton grew impatient. He didn't want to just study Aristotle's theories about how the world works and Ptolemy's model for the heavens. He wanted to find out for himself what actually made the Sun rise and set. Instead of someone else's description, he wanted a proper explanation.

Learning for himself

So Newton wrote a long list of the subjects he wanted to study – ranging from time, **eternity** and space through to vision, colours and sounds – and he set about studying them by himself.

He read with interest the ideas of more recent philosophers. Copernicus and Galileo's books were still banned by the Catholic Church, but their work was gaining support across Europe. Newton liked their ideas but he felt they needed explaining. He wanted to know *how* the Earth could physically achieve the rotations and orbits it's supposed to. And what about the other planets? How could *they* make such astonishing movements?

The apple and the Moon

Newton's major breakthrough came when he was forced home in 1666 because of the threat of the highly **contagious** and deadly bubonic plague.

In the garden at Woolsthorpe Manor, there was a small apple orchard. Newton later described his thoughts on seeing an apple fall.

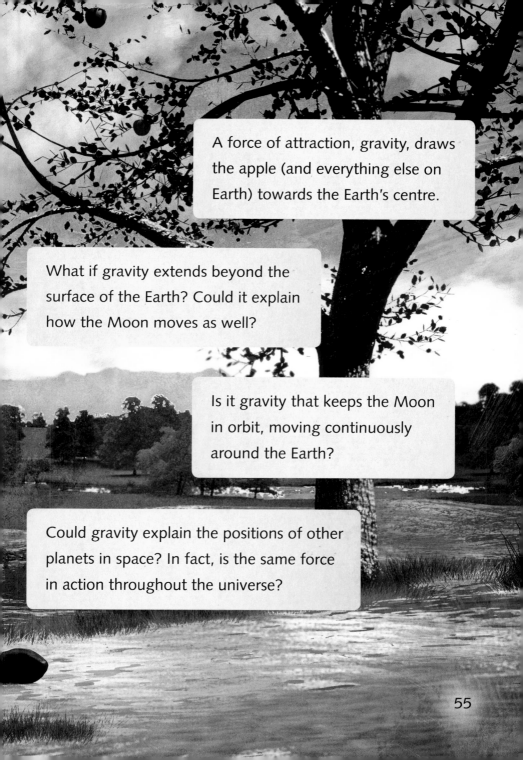

A force of attraction, gravity, draws the apple (and everything else on Earth) towards the Earth's centre.

What if gravity extends beyond the surface of the Earth? Could it explain how the Moon moves as well?

Is it gravity that keeps the Moon in orbit, moving continuously around the Earth?

Could gravity explain the positions of other planets in space? In fact, is the same force in action throughout the universe?

Keeping quiet

Newton didn't have these thoughts in a sudden **Eureka!**
moment. More likely, it was a gradual process of discovery.
The idea that there was a force called gravity that pulled objects
to Earth wasn't new. But the idea that gravity could be
a universal force, acting in the same way across the universe,
was revolutionary.

To begin with, Newton kept his thoughts to himself.
He was a private man who didn't easily share his ideas.
In any case, this was just one of many subjects that he was
interested in researching.

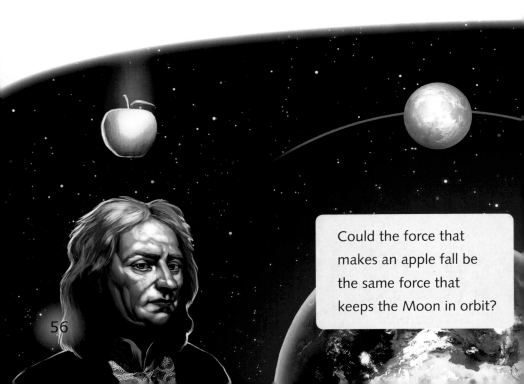

Could the force that
makes an apple fall be
the same force that
keeps the Moon in orbit?

Back to Cambridge

When the threat of the plague had gone, Newton returned to Cambridge, where he soon became Professor of Mathematics. Seven years went by and other people started asking questions about how gravity might affect objects in orbit.

Partly out of rivalry and partly out of curiosity, Newton returned to his earlier thoughts about the apple and the Moon. Could he somehow use gravity to calculate the positions and movements of celestial bodies across the entire universe?

Trinity College,
Cambridge

How does gravity work?

Newton needed a formula – a rule that could be used to work out the force of gravity in any situation.

He worked out that every object in the universe pulls on every other object. The strength of the pull between two objects – the force of gravity between them – depends on only two things: the mass of the objects (how much matter or "stuff" they are made of) and the distance they are apart.

Objects with a greater mass have a greater force of gravity.

The further away two objects are from each other, the weaker the force of gravity between them.

Earth has a greater mass than an apple; that's why the apple falls to Earth rather than the other way round. But Earth also has a greater mass than the Moon. So why doesn't the Moon fall to Earth?

It's partly because the distance between the Moon and the Earth is so large the pull of gravity between them is weaker. It's also because while the Earth is pulling on the Moon, the Moon is also pulling on the Earth, and the constant pull in opposite directions keeps them roughly the same distance apart. But as the Moon's pull is weaker, it's the Moon that orbits the Earth rather than the Earth orbiting the Moon.

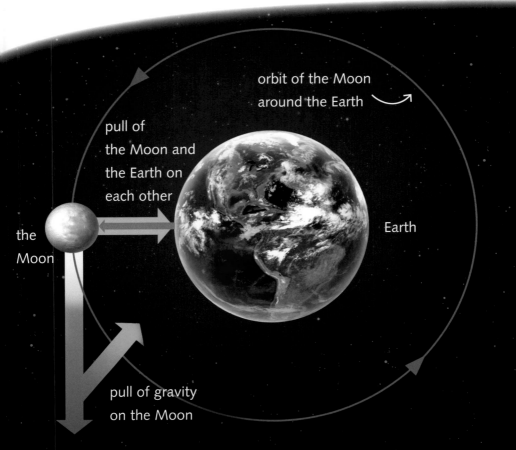

orbit of the Moon
around the Earth

pull of
the Moon and
the Earth on
each other

the
Moon

Earth

pull of gravity
on the Moon

The Moon would move here, but the Earth's gravity
is pulling it in another direction

The law of gravity

Newton was able to prove the relationship between force, mass and distance by matching it with the actual movements of the celestial bodies. He called his theory the "universal law of gravity".

In science, a "law" is a general statement that's based on the results of a series of experiments. The statement must hold true every time the experiment is performed under the same conditions. A "universal law" is a statement that holds true across the whole universe.

The laws of motion

Newton also developed three laws of motion, building on the works of Galileo and Kepler. These laws described how objects move under a force such as gravity. He then used his laws of gravity and motion to study the movement of the planets.

By observing the effects of gravity between one object and another, and by applying his laws, Newton was able to roughly work out their masses. He worked out that the Sun had a much greater mass than the Earth and the other planets. That explained why the Sun was at the centre – because its gravitational pull was stronger, so it pulled all the other planets into orbit around it.

the planets rotating
around the Sun

Moving in ellipses

So what shape do planets in orbit make? Ptolemy, Copernicus and Galileo all believed that they moved in perfect circles. But the circles didn't match the movements seen in the sky, so they'd had to add epicycles – little circles within the circles.

Kepler, the astronomer who'd encouraged Galileo to speak out about the Earth moving around the Sun, had developed his own theory on the movement of the planets. He believed that they moved in regular oval shapes, called ellipses, instead of in circles and epicycles. While his theory provided an accurate match for *how* the planets move in the sky, he couldn't explain *why* they moved in this way.

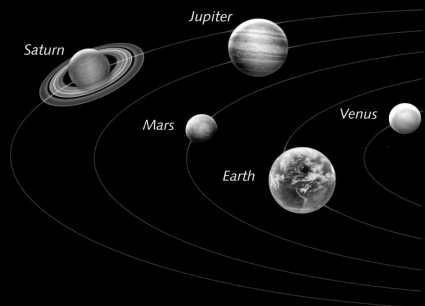

Newton had the answer: because of gravity. And when he used his law of gravity to calculate the pull on the planets as they orbited the Sun, he proved that the shape they moved in was indeed an ellipse.

When the astronomer Edmond Halley visited Newton in 1684, he was astounded by how much Newton had already worked out – and had kept to himself. Halley eventually persuaded Newton to write down his discoveries and to share them with others. In 1687, Newton's work on gravity and motion was finally published in a book.

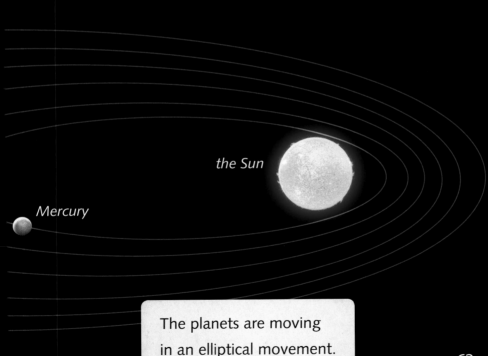

the Sun

Mercury

The planets are moving in an elliptical movement.

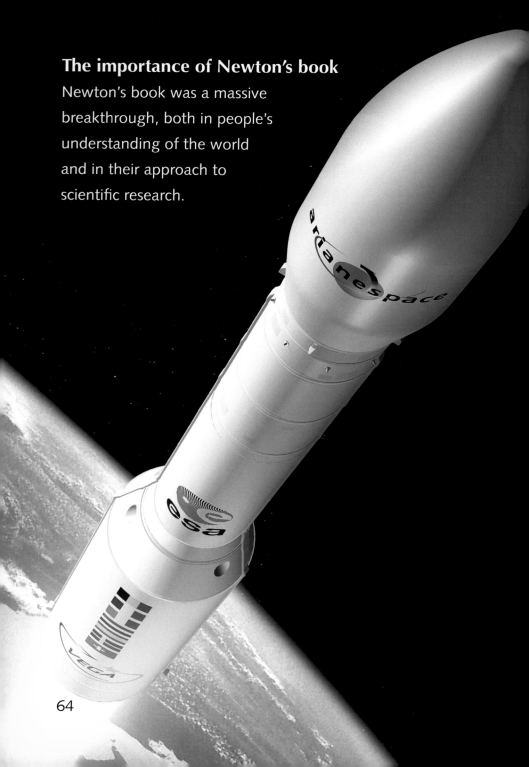

The importance of Newton's book

Newton's book was a massive
breakthrough, both in people's
understanding of the world
and in their approach to
scientific research.

Newton completed the revolution that Copernicus had started. He provided a consistent, physical explanation of how the planets, including the Earth, are kept in orbit around the Sun.

He was the first person to propose a set of laws that applied across the universe. He ended forever the view held by Aristotle and Ptolemy that the heavens were perfect and unchanging and that the Earth had its own, separate rules.

Not only did Newton describe *how* the celestial bodies behaved, he also explained *why* they behaved in that way – because of gravity. His laws gave the world tools to study space more accurately, and his calculations enabled later scientists to work out how to travel into space.

Fame and power

Newton became famous throughout Europe. In 1703, he was elected President of the Royal Society – a group of important scholars interested in finding out more about the natural world – and in 1705 he was knighted. Sir Isaac Newton died in 1727, at the age of 84.

Space science today

Moving through space

After Newton's discoveries, no one could deny that the Earth
moved around the Sun. His theory of gravity even explained
why we don't feel a rush of air as the Earth moves through space.
Gravity pulls the air around us towards Earth, so as the Earth
is moving, the air is moving along with it.

Newton had explained the basic structure of our Solar System,
but there was still so much more to find out.

Mercury

Venus

Earth

Mars

Space science today

Finding Uranus ...

In 1781, the astronomer William Hershel, through careful
observation, realised that one of the stars in the night sky was
actually another planet. He'd discovered the seventh planet in
our Solar System, Uranus. Uranus is visible to the naked eye,
but it's so dim and its orbit is so slow that no one had noticed it
could be a planet before.

... and Neptune

In the 1840s, several people realised that Uranus moved in a strange way: sometimes going faster, sometimes going slower. Using Newton's law of gravity, they worked out that another large mass – an undiscovered planet – was pulling on Uranus. They calculated where in the sky that planet might be, and when a team of astronomers investigated, they discovered Neptune, the eighth planet in our Solar System.

Jupiter

Neptune

Uranus

Saturn

Beyond our Solar System

Until the 1920s, people thought our Solar System *was* the universe. They didn't realise that our Solar System is just one of many. They thought that the stars all lie at roughly the same distance from Earth, when in fact some of them are vast clusters of stars, lying much further away than the stars they appear alongside.

These vast clusters are called galaxies. To the naked eye they look like fuzzy stars, but in 1922 an American astronomer called Edwin Hubble studied one through a very powerful telescope and saw that it was made up of lots of individual stars. With this discovery came the realisation that there are many galaxies in the universe. Our Solar System is part of the Milky Way galaxy, but the Milky Way is only a tiny fragment of the universe.

the Milky Way

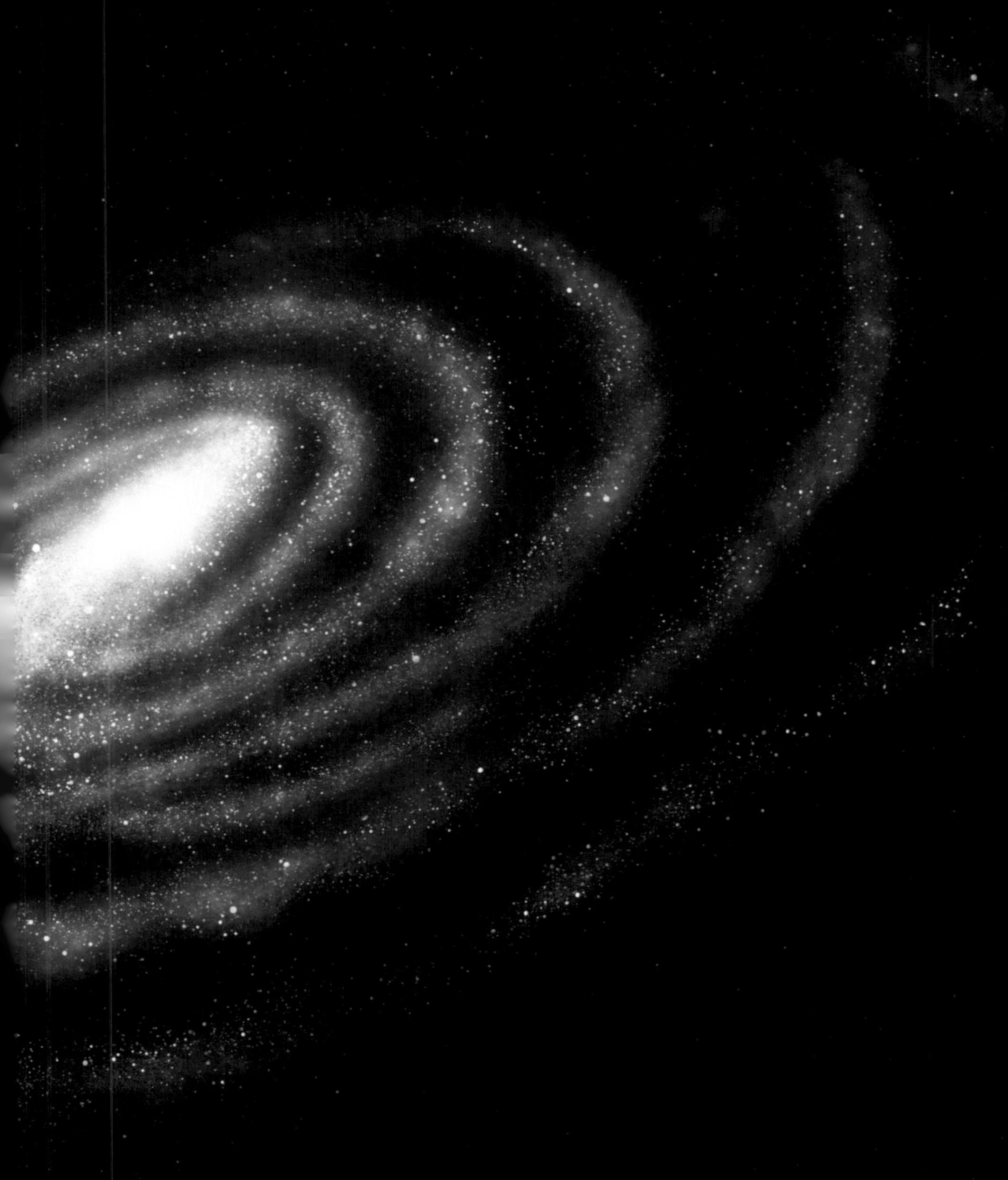

Measuring the stars

Edwin Hubble wanted to work out just how far these other galaxies are from Earth. There's a type of star, known as a variable star, that slowly **pulses** in the sky, shining bright then dim then bright then dim. Hubble studied the changing brightness of variable stars over time and used his results to work out how far they must be from Earth.

The distances involved are huge; so far that it's easier to measure them in **light years** rather than in miles or kilometres.

Light years away

Hubble worked out that our nearest galaxy is 25,000 light years away. That means it's taken 25,000 years for its light to reach us. And if it's taken that long to reach us, then what we're seeing isn't how the galaxy looks now, but how it looked 25,000 years ago!

Amazingly, when we look into space, we're actually looking back in time.

The Hubble Space Telescope

In 1990 a large telescope, named the Hubble Space Telescope after Edwin Hubble, was launched into Earth's orbit.

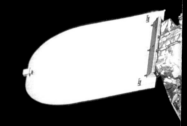

Because it sits outside the Earth's atmosphere, it has a much clearer view into space than telescopes on Earth. Using Hubble, space scientists can look so far into space that they can see how stars and galaxies were forming billions of years ago.

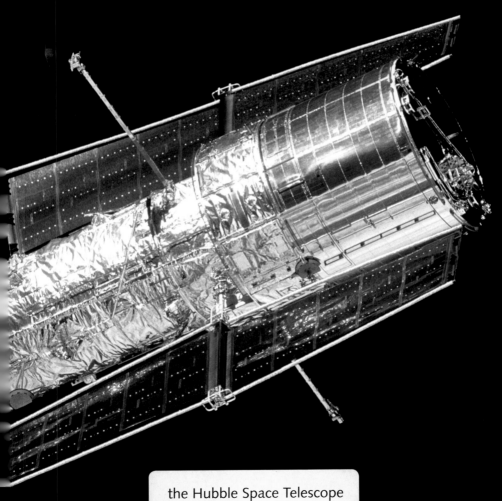

the Hubble Space Telescope

Back to the beginning

The furthest image recorded by Hubble shows galaxies 13.2 billion light years away. This means Hubble is giving us a view of the universe from 13.2 billion years ago.

Nebula

Space scientists believe that the universe is roughly 13.7 billion years old. They hope that future telescopes more powerful than Hubble, such as the James Webb Space Telescope, will be able to see right back to the beginning of the universe.

the James Webb Space Telescope

Space exploration

Space scientists don't just study the history of space though, they're continually exploring what else might be out there.

So far, the furthest humans have travelled is to the Moon, but there are plans for astronauts to visit planet Mars in the next 20 years. Unmanned spacecraft have been much further. The Voyager 1 space probe has been travelling in space for over 35 years. It's currently somewhere at the edge of our Solar System, still sending amazing images back to Earth.

Looking for alien life

One of the things space probes look for is evidence of life on other planets. In our galaxy alone there are billions of planets.

It seems possible that at least one of them might have the right conditions for life to exist, although no one yet knows what a living thing on another planet might look like.

Understanding the pattern

The pattern of stars, planets and galaxies that we see in the sky has remained virtually the same throughout the history of mankind. Only our understanding of what we see has changed, and a significant part of that understanding we owe to the early space scientists for daring to think differently.

a computer-generated image of a space probe on Mars

Glossary

axis	a real or imaginary line through the centre of an object, around which the object turns
BCE	before the common era (the same as BC)
contagious	can be spread from person to person
eclipses	the moments when our view of the Sun, the Moon or a planet is blocked by another body in the universe
eternity	time that lasts forever without a beginning or an end
Eureka	based on a Greek word meaning, "I have found it!"
fine-tune	make final improvements
house arrest	being imprisoned at home, rather than in prison
light years	a unit of length equal to the distance that light travels in one year (nine trillion and 460 billion kilometres)
logic	a way of solving a problem by thinking it through carefully
magnification	making something appear larger
orbiting	moving around something
philosophers	people who study the truth about life
pious	showing love and respect for a god
prestigious	admired and important in the world
pulses	regular beats
space probes	spacecraft that visit planets and send information back to Earth without astronauts on board
supernova	a very bright object that results from the explosion of a star

Index

Aristotle   4, 8, 9, 11, 32, 35, 40, 52, 65

Astronomy   13, 14, 29, 32, 52

Copernicus   4, 12-29, 34, 40, 42, 53, 62, 65

Earth   2, 3, 4, 6, 7, 8, 9, 10, 11, 17, 18, 20, 22, 23, 24, 25, 29, 34, 38, 40, 41, 42, 44, 53, 55, 56, 58, 59, 60, 62, 65, 66, 68, 70, 71, 74

epicycles   10, 11, 22, 62

galaxies   2, 68, 70, 71, 72, 75

Galileo   5, 30-47, 48, 53, 60, 62

gravity   55, 56, 57, 58, 59, 60, 63, 65, 66, 67

Jupiter   6, 9, 38, 40, 62, 67

Kepler   34, 35, 60, 62

Mars   6, 7, 9, 41, 62, 66, 74, 75

Mercury   6, 9, 41, 63, 66

Milky Way   38, 68

Moon   6, 7, 8, 9, 14, 17, 20, 38, 40, 54, 55, 56, 57, 58, 59, 74

Neptune   67

Newton   5, 48-65, 66, 67

planet(s)   2, 3, 4, 6, 7, 8, 10, 11, 14, 18, 20, 22, 23, 38, 40, 53, 55, 60, 61, 62, 63, 65, 66, 67, 74, 75

Ptolemy   4, 10, 11, 13, 16, 17, 23, 24, 35, 40, 44, 52, 62, 65

Saturn   6, 9, 41, 62, 67

Solar System   2, 3, 66, 67, 68, 74

spyglass   36, 37

star(s)   3, 6, 7, 8, 11, 13, 14, 16, 17, 20, 24, 25, 35, 38, 66, 68, 70, 71, 75

Sun   2, 6, 7, 8, 9, 17, 18, 20, 21, 22, 23, 29, 40, 41, 42, 44, 46, 49, 52, 60, 61, 62, 63, 65, 66

supernova   35

telescope   6, 18, 35, 37, 38, 39, 40, 41, 44, 68, 70, 71, 73

universe   2, 4, 5, 7, 9, 11, 13, 17, 20, 23, 26, 29, 30, 34, 40, 41, 42, 43, 44, 46, 55, 56, 57, 58, 60, 65, 68, 72, 73

Uranus   66, 67

Venus   6, 9, 40, 41, 62, 66

Space through time

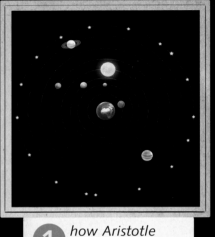

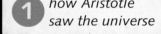

1 how Aristotle saw the universe

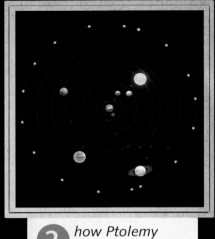

2 how Ptolemy saw the universe

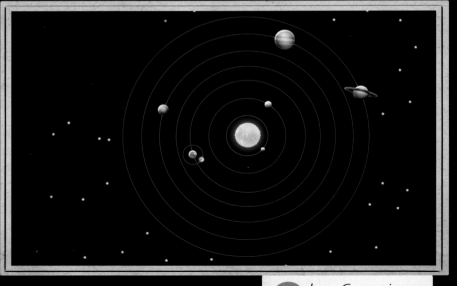

3 how Copernicus saw the universe

4 *how Galileo*
saw the universe

5 *how Newton*
saw the universe

Ideas for reading

Written by Clare Dowdall, PhD
Lecturer and Primary Literacy Consultant

Learning objectives: check that the book makes sense, discuss understanding and explore the meaning of words in context; ask questions to improve understanding; summarise the main ideas drawn from more than one paragraph, identify key details that support the main ideas; retrieve, record and present information from non-fiction; note and develop initial ideas, drawing on reading and research where necessary

Curriculum links: Science

Interest words: axis, eclipses, eternity, Eureka, fine-tune, light years, logic, magnification, orbiting, philosophers, pious, prestigious, pulses, space probes, supernova

Resources: whiteboard and pens, materials to create a timeline, ICT

Getting started

This book can be read over two or more reading sessions.

- Read the title and help children to pronounce the names. Ask children for any ideas about who Copernicus, Galileo and Newton were and what they discovered. Collect ideas on a whiteboard.

- Turn to the contents. Read them together and ask children to discuss what they think space science involves. Ask children to briefly explain what they know about space, e.g. two fast facts each.

Reading and responding

- Ask children to read pp2–11 to find out what space science is and how space is organised. Provide the key words: planets and moons, Solar System, galaxy, universe. Challenge children to arrange them to reflect how they co-exist (p2).

80